NEW BELIEVER'S GUIDE TO
How to Share Your Faith

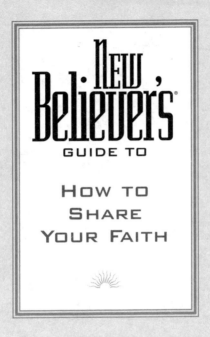

New Believer's®

GUIDE TO

HOW TO
SHARE
YOUR FAITH

GREG LAURIE

TYNDALE HOUSE PUBLISHERS, INC.
WHEATON, ILLINOIS

Library of Congress Cataloging-in-Publication Data

Laurie, Greg.
  [How to share your faith]
  New believer's guide to how to share your faith / by Greg
Laurie.
    p. cm.
Originally published: How to share your faith. ©1999.
  ISBN 0-8423-5579-0
1. Witness bearing (Christianity) I. Title
BV4520 .L338 2002
248′.5—dc21   2001008484

Printed in the United States of America

06   05   04   03   02
6   5   4   3   2   1

Table of Contents

INTRODUCTION

On more than one occasion when I was growing up, I remember hearing people say to me rather scoldingly, "Greg, will you grow up?!" It was their way of saying that I was too much of a goof-off or was behaving like a child.

I've always been a bit of a prankster (I guess I still am), and I like to have fun. It seems to me that some people are a little bit too "grown-up" before their time. They are so responsible, so mature, so dependable, already telling all the other kids what to do by the age of 5.

I figure, however, that you should enjoy your childhood because you have to grow up soon enough. Unfortunately, it seems that many of us don't fully appreciate our childhoods until much later in life. But by that time, of course, we can't go back. There is a time to "grow up," to no longer be childish.

We can and must, however, remain "childlike" in our faith. Jesus said, "I assure you, unless you turn from your sins and become as little children, you will never get into the Kingdom of Heaven. Therefore, anyone who becomes as humble as this little child is the greatest in the Kingdom of Heaven" (Matthew 18:3-4, NLT).

Notice that I did not say that we should be "childish" in our faith, but rather "child-like." This simply means that we as believers must humble ourselves, realize that we don't have all the answers, and in childlike dependence, trust in Christ, even when we don't have all the answers. Being childlike means maintaining that sense of wonder and awe at God's power, creation, love.

But as the years pass, our faith should deepen and grow. We must grow up spiritually. It is really sad when somebody never does grow up spiritually.

The Apostle Paul points that out in 1 Corinthians 14:20: "Dear brothers and sisters, don't be childish in your understanding of these things. Be innocent as babies when it comes to evil, but be mature and wise in understanding matters of this kind."

There is nothing wrong with being a "spiritual baby" when you are still new in the faith. But if, after you have some years under your belt, you are still behaving like a little child, that is not a good thing.

As the author of Hebrews reminds us: "So let us stop going over the basics of Christianity again and again. Let us go on instead and become mature in our understanding. Surely we don't need to start all over again with the importance of turning away from evil deeds and placing our faith in God" (Hebrews 6:1, NLT).

That is why I have written this series of books for new believers. They are designed for people like you—new believers, those who are novices when it comes to faith and spiritual growth. These books are designed to help you grow up spiritually and become a mature follower of Jesus Christ.

This book that you hold in your hand focuses on how to share your newfound faith. You may feel so new to this whole "Christian" thing that you're not able to tell anyone else how to become a Christian. But you're wrong. You're ready to share because it's not all up to you. With the Spirit within you, you're already a shining light for Christ. Now you just need to put some words with it!

This book will give you some "whys" and some "how tos." As Jesus sent his disciples out to "fish for people" (Matthew 4:19), so this whole process of sharing your faith has a lot in common with fishing. I'll help you with a few hints, give some guidelines about the basic gospel message, and offer some steps that will help you feel confident in leading another person to Christ.

As you will discover, I use lots of stories and passages from Scripture. That is because there can be no spiritual growth in a person's life without a steady diet of the Word of God.

So let's grab our gear and head out to the fishing hole!

—*Greg Laurie*

1

THE BURDEN

I was as green as they come, as far as sharing the gospel went. Yet there I was, a young teenager out on the beach, looking for someone to talk to about my newfound faith in Christ. It did not turn out the way I had expected.

I was only two weeks old in my commitment to Christ. I didn't know much about Christian living or the Bible, but I had heard that I should go out and share the gospel with others. So one day I went down to the beach—the same beach where I used to make a point of avoiding any Bible-toting Christians who might try convert me.

Now here I was—a bona fide member of the "Soul Patrol"—out prowling for unbelievers to convert. But I wasn't exactly full of confidence. In fact, my main goal was to find someone who wouldn't argue or get angry at me. I thought if an unbeliever just ignored me or walked away, that would be fine.

Eventually, I spotted a middle-aged lady who looked about the age of my mom. I figured she might be somewhat sympathetic to me.

When I walked up to her, my voice trembled with nervousness. "Uh, excuse me," I said, fumbling for the right words. "Can I talk to you about something?"

She said, "Sure. What about?"

"Well, about, like, God—and stuff," I answered. (Remember, I was still a teenager.)

To my amazement, she said, "Go ahead. Sit down. Talk to me."

I then pulled out a copy of an evangelistic tract I had stuffed in my pocket for a moment like this. I was so new in the faith that I hadn't even memorized the plan of salvation, so I just read through the entire booklet verbatim. The whole time I read, I was shaking like a leaf and thinking, *This isn't going to work. Why am I doing this? This is not going to reach her.*

But the woman continued to patiently listen to what I was saying—rather, reading.

When I got to a part in the booklet that said, "Is there any good reason why you should not accept Jesus Christ right now?" I realized that I should direct this question to the woman. I hesitated. Feeling awkward, I looked up and asked her, "Uh, is there any good reason why you should not accept Jesus Christ right now?"

"No," she replied.

"Okay," I said, slightly confused. "Then that would mean that you *do* want to accept Jesus Christ right now?"

With a look of quiet resolve, she answered, "Yes, I would."

I was shocked. For a moment I didn't know what to do. I had only planned for failure. Frantically I searched the tract for some kind of prayer in which to lead a person who wanted to invite Christ into his or her life. After what seemed an eternity, I finally found one. In the most reverent tone I could muster, I said, "Let's bow our heads for a word of prayer."

Even as she prayed after me, I was still thinking, *This is not going to work.*

After we were done, the woman looked up at me and said, "Something just happened to me!"

And at that moment something happened to me, too: I got a taste of what it was like to be used by God. I knew—even at that point at that young age—that no matter what I did in life, I wanted to continue to share the gospel.

Burdened for Unbelievers

Any effective sharing of one's faith will always begin with a God-given burden for lost people—those who don't know Christ. And if some of us today were brutally honest, we would have to say that we don't have that burden. If we did, quite frankly, I think many of us would do more than we do.

"But I'm not qualified or an expert on theology," some might protest.

Let me put it this way: Let's say that you are walking

down the street and hear the screams of a woman. You turn to see what the problem is, and she points to a burning house and hysterically cries that her little baby is inside. You realize that you have only moments before the entire house will be engulfed with flames.

Would you simply walk away, reasoning that it was her child and not yours? Not likely.

Would you try to quiet her down and tell her to wait until the professionals arrive? Possibly, but again, not likely.

Would you risk your own life and try to get into that building and save that child? I would hope so.

A fate even worse than that awaits those who do not know Christ. For them, the fire is not temporary but eternal. Do we honestly care? People can tell if we really do when we talk to them about our faith in Christ. They can sense if we are simply doing it out of duty and our heart is not really in it. I have seen Christians share the gospel in an almost mechanical way. They have their canned statements and answers. They are not really engaged. This will ultimately defeat their own purpose.

You can talk about love all you want. You can cite the various Greek words the Bible uses to describe it. You can even quote numerous passages from Scripture to prove the importance of it. But the best thing you can do is to demonstrate it as you share your faith. To do that effectively, you need a God-given burden.

Burdened to Get Involved

We need to have a burden like Jesus had for the people of Jerusalem. Scripture describes his heartfelt burden as he looked out over Jerusalem one day and wept, saying, "O Jerusalem, Jerusalem, the one who kills the prophets and stones those who are sent to her! How often I wanted to gather your children together, as a hen gathers her chicks under her wings, but you were not willing!" (Matthew 23:37).

The apostle Paul echoes that sentiment in Romans 9:2-3: "I have great sorrow and continual grief in my heart. For I could wish that I myself were accursed from Christ for my brethren, my countrymen according to the flesh."

No wonder Paul had such a powerful and effective ministry. He cared!

Nehemiah is another classic illustration of a man who was genuinely touched with the needs of the lost. As cupbearer to the king of Persia, he was in a position of great power and influence. While possessing this status and prestige, he was also a Jew—one of the many who had been in exile away from Jerusalem.

Nehemiah could have easily kicked back and set up house on easy street. One day his brother came back from a visit to Jerusalem and told Nehemiah about the destruction he had seen. The once proud and erect walls of the city were now simply heaps of charred rubble. Nehemiah recognized that these walls were a symbol of a people who once stood with God, separated from the pagan nations around them. But now they lay in ruin. This revelation so broke Nehemiah's heart that he wept. Yet after Nehemiah's weeping came working. After his despair came determination.

He could have rationalized his way out of personally doing anything by saying, "I'm no priest or prophet. Let them take care of it! Besides, if I speak up, I may jeopardize my coveted position with the king. What good would that do?"

But Nehemiah realized that he, a layman, could make a difference. So he prayed, and he obtained permission from the king to go and personally assess the damage. After Nehemiah did that, he drafted a plan and acted upon it (Nehemiah 1–2).

It's not enough to only plan. It's not even enough to only pray. We have to move when God tells us to move. When Moses was on the shore of the Red Sea with the Egyptian army in hot pursuit, the Lord said to Moses, "Why are you crying out to me? Tell the people to get moving!" (Exodus 14:15, NLT).

There is a time to pray and a time to move—a time to sow and a time to reap. But it all starts with a God-given burden for lost people. Alexander McClaren said, "You tell me the depth of a Christian's compassion, and I will tell you the measure of his usefulness." To quote the great British pastor C. H. Spurgeon,

"Winners of souls must first be weepers of souls."
This is essential to effectively sharing your faith.

Gripped with Urgency

I would suggest the reason many Christians have
never led another person to Christ is that we have
never really asked a person that pivotal question:
"Would you like to accept Jesus Christ into your life
as your personal Savior?" We chicken out at the last
minute. *What if they say no?* we may wonder. Our real
fear might actually be, *What if they say yes?*

If they do say yes—and I believe that if you are ac-
tively sharing your faith, you will eventually get such
an answer—it will be one of the greatest joys you will
ever know this side of heaven. Just think—a person's
eternal destiny has changed! A person who had been
on his way to hell is now going to heaven. A person
who was empty and lonely is now fulfilled and complete—all because you took the time to share the gospel message.

Yet, so many of us give up too easily. We may ask
our unbelieving friends, "Do you want to come to
church with me?"

"No," they flatly reply.

"Okay, never mind," you say, dropping the subject
and perhaps feeling slightly relieved.

How can we give up so easily? Do we really believe
what we claim to believe? Are we convinced of the reality of a heaven and a hell? Do we actually accept that

the wages of sin really are death? If so, how can we be so casual about telling others?

Many years ago in England, a criminal named Charles Peace was arrested. He was a burglar, a forger, and he was guilty of double murder. He was condemned to death for his crimes. As he was making his way to the gallows on the day of his execution, a chaplain walked by his side. This minister was simply "going through the motions," speaking coldly of the importance of faith and belief. In the course of his oft-repeated speech, the minister mentioned the power of Jesus Christ to save from sin.

Suddenly the criminal spun around, looked the chaplain in the eye, and exclaimed, "Do you believe that? Do you really believe that? If I believed that, I would willingly crawl across England on broken glass to tell men it was true." If we really believe what we are sharing, we should be gripped with the urgency of the message.

I want to encourage you and help you to see that God can indeed use you to bring others into his kingdom.

Sharing, Not Converting

Without question, conversion is the work of the Holy Spirit. Jesus says, "No one can come to Me unless the Father who sent Me draws him" (John 6:44). Paul also reminds us, "Neither he who plants nor he who waters is anything, but only God, who makes things grow. The man who plants and the man who waters have one purpose, and each will be rewarded according to his own labor" (1 Corinthians 3:7-8, NIV).

There is nothing you or I can do to make a person convert. I've heard Billy Graham tell the story of a very inebriated man who happened to be on the same flight as the famed evangelist. Hearing Billy was on board, this drunken man demanded to speak with him. The flight attendants tried to keep the man in his seat, but he would not be satisfied until he had spoken with Billy himself. Hearing about this, Billy got out of his seat and greeted the man.

The drunken man said, "Billy, I'm glad to meet you! I'm one of your converts!"

Billy thought to himself, *He must be one of my converts. He certainly isn't one of the Lord's.*

Only God can bring about a true conversion. Sometimes we get to a certain place in our gospel presentation where we may feel compelled to apply a little pressure. We want to close the deal—possibly before it is ready to happen. Remember, our job is to clearly and accurately present the gospel message, leaving the results to God. As Sergeant Friday of the classic TV program *Dragnet* used to say, "Just the facts, ma'am." Of course, you must be ready to "pull in the net" if the person is ready. If that individual is not at that point, however, leave the timing to God.

Used by God

Statistics tell us that 95 percent of all Christians have never led another person to Christ. Are you in that massive percentage? Or are you in that "elite few" who have had the privilege of helping a person pass from darkness to light?

I believe that God can and will use you to lead others to himself. I do not think that bringing others to Christ is only the work of a select few. Granted, some have been specifically called to be evangelists. That is a gift that comes from God, and it is not limited to those who may hold evangelistic crusades (though it obviously includes them). It is a calling that I have personally seen in the lives of those who are in their seventies as well as those who are still very young. These individuals simply have a special way of freely sharing the gospel with astounding results.

But don't let that discourage you. For although biblical principles will enable you to more effectively tell others about Jesus Christ, you must first understand that there is both a right and wrong way to share the gospel. Second, you will learn that certain essentials need to be in place for the gospel to be the gospel.

2

ARE WE THE OBSTACLE?

God Works Through Imperfect People

It's been said that there are two reasons people do not go to church: (1) They don't know a Christian, or (2) they do.

Sometimes in our inexperience or overzealous ways, we are our own worst enemies. We console ourselves with the verse that says, "Blessed are those who are persecuted for righteousness' sake" (Matthew 5:10), when in reality we are sometimes "persecuted" for being obnoxious, strange, or just plain weird!

Many times, unbelievers are not rejecting the gospel itself as much as they are rejecting the way it is presented. They don't necessarily object to what is inside the box; they just don't like its wrapping.

That is not to say that there is no offense in the message of the gospel. Indeed, it can and will be offensive at times. Acknowledging a holy God and a place of eternal judgment will bother and even offend some people. Yet at the same time, let's make sure it is the gospel they are offended by instead of some bizarre thing an alleged follower of Christ says or does.

I must admit that it really is a mystery that God has chosen to use people as the primary communicators of his truth in the first place—and that he has chosen preaching as his primary method of communication! Romans 10:14-15 says, "How can they call on him to save them unless they believe in him? And how can they believe in him if they have never heard about him? And how can they hear about him unless someone tells them? And how will anyone go and tell them without being sent? That is what the Scriptures mean when they say, 'How beautiful are the feet of those who bring good news!' " (NLT).

The apostle Paul reiterates this message in 1 Corinthians 1:21: "Since, in the wisdom of God, the world through wisdom did not know God, it pleased God through the foolishness of the message preached to save those who believe."

That verse does not say that God uses foolish preaching (of which there is plenty, unfortunately) to save those who believe; nor does it say that preaching a "foolish" message (though it will be perceived as such to some) will effectively do the work. For again Scripture reminds us, "The message of the cross is foolishness to those who are perishing" (1 Corinthians 1:18).

Paul is essentially pointing out how simple, unexpected, and unbelievable it is that through basic verbal communication (backed by the power of the Spirit and a godly life), a person's eternal destiny can be instantaneously changed! It seems to me that it would be much more effective for God to roll away the heavens, poke his head through the clouds and say, "Hello, humanity! I'm God, and you are not. So I strongly suggest that you all believe in me right now." Somehow I think that would get a good response. Or he could send thousands of angels in all of their splendor to proclaim the gospel. But he has not chosen to work that way. Instead, he has primarily chosen to use people like you and me.

A Lesson from the *Titanic*

Through the help of Hollywood and the passing of time, we have all come to know the story of the sinking of the *Titanic*. One of the things that makes this tragedy so captivating is the realization that the story could have been different had the ship's captain and crew not made so many disastrous decisions and mistakes.

We've learned how those in charge repeatedly and flagrantly ignored the warnings of ice ahead. We know that the captain tried to steer the ship around the fatal iceberg instead of hitting it head-on, which, with the advantage of hindsight, would have been the better choice. We also know that there were not enough lifeboats on board. One of the greatest tragedies of the *Titanic* story is that when the massive ship went under, many of those lifeboats were only half full. Those in the lifeboats could hear the screams of the people (many of them their husbands and sons), yet not one boat went back until one long hour had passed.

They returned after the screams had subsided. They rowed back to the people only when they felt it was safe. But it was too late.

Listen! The screams of those who are without Christ can be heard. They may not even realize the severity of their situation yet, but they cry out to us. We must go and pull them into the lifeboat!

To quote the wise C. H. Spurgeon again, this is what we must remember when we bring the gospel to those who do not yet know him:

> The Holy Spirit will move them by first moving you. If you can rest without their being saved, they will rest, too. But if you are filled with an agony for them, if you cannot bear that they should be lost, you will soon find that they are uneasy, too. I hope you will get into such a state that you will dream about your child or your hearer perishing for lack of Christ, and start up at once and begin to cry, "Oh God, give me converts or I will die." Then you will have converts.

Distortions of the Message

Some years ago, I was walking down the main street of Waikiki in Hawaii. I saw a man standing on one of the corners with a rather large sign. Emblazoned on the sign were the words *The Wages of Sin Is Death!* It also had some flames painted on it, no doubt for effect.

Yelling at the top of his voice to every passerby, the overly zealous street preacher shouted such things as, "You're gonna burn!" "God will judge you, sinner!" and "Repent or perish!" The things he was saying certainly had a ring of truth to them. At the same time, there was no love or compassion in his delivery. In fact, it almost seemed as though he took some kind of perverse pleasure in yelling this out to people.

So I walked up to him and tried to get his attention. "Excuse me—"

He continued screaming at the people passing by, "Repent, ye sinners!"

"Pardon me."

He continued yelling. Finally I got his attention. "What do you want?" he barked.

"Well," I said, "I'm a Christian, too, but I was thinking that you are really only giving half of the gospel message out here tonight. It is true that the wages of sin is death, but I'm sure you're aware of the fact that the rest of that very verse says, 'But the gift of God is eternal life through Jesus Christ our Lord.' Why don't you put that message on the other side of your sign and turn it around every now and then so people get the whole picture?"

Then he screamed at me and told me that I was

going to hell, too! It is sad when people misrepresent God like that.

How Not to be an Obstacle

Does your heart ache to share the hope of the gospel with those around you? Do you have a burden for those who do not yet know the Lord? Do you want to be a part of the solution, and not part of the problem? You might pause right now and pray something like this:

> Lord, from this moment forward, I pray that you will give me a burden and concern for people who do not yet know you. Help me to see them as you do. Help me to care enough to share your gospel with them. Give me that burden for the lost like you and the apostle Paul and Nehemiah had. Lord, I admit that at times I am afraid to step out. Please give me a new boldness to do that. I thank you in advance, Lord. In Jesus' name I pray, amen.

If you pray a prayer like that and mean it, you may never be the same again—and, I dare say, this world in which we live may not be either.

3

PATIENCE AND MORE PATIENCE

Let's Go Fishing!

Sharing the gospel is a lot like going fishing. In fact, Jesus used that very metaphor. Matthew's Gospel tells us that Jesus was walking by the Sea of Galilee when he "saw two brothers, Simon called Peter, and Andrew his brother, casting a net into the sea; for they were fishermen. He said to them, 'Follow Me, and I will make you fishers of men' " (Matthew 4:18-19).

Jesus has called all of us to "go fishing for men," too! A more literal translation of that phrase would be "I will make you catch men alive." The actual Greek verb used for *catch* is unique, and it occurs in only one other place in the Bible. In that instance, Paul tells us to be patient with those who oppose the truth, "that they may come to their senses and escape the snare of the devil, having been taken captive [caught alive] by him to do his will" (2 Timothy 2:26).

Here Scripture presents a striking contrast. Either the devil will catch men alive, or we will. So, are you ready to go fishing? Let's consider a few traits that make for a good fisherman.

Learn to Wait

It takes time to catch fish. You must learn to wait—and wait and wait! Some years ago I had the opportunity to go fishing for king salmon on the Kenai River in Alaska. I was told that it took an average of fifty hours to pull one of these bad boys in, so I was prepared for a long wait. I got a few pulls on my line, then all of a sudden, *Wham!* That line got a tug so hard you would have thought that I had a great white shark on the end of it! Okay, so I exaggerate. Would you believe a sixty-five-pound king salmon? For that is exactly what it was.

I reeled in as rapidly as I could, pulling so hard on my pole that it bent over almost parallel with itself. I thought it would snap at any moment. The rod held, though it quickly stripped, and I was just pulling for dear life to get this giant beast of a fish on board. I got him right to the edge of our boat, and he poked his massive head out of the water. We could not believe his size! Our guide put his net into the water and almost had him when that monster king salmon just snapped the line like a piece of thread.

That was it. I was really disappointed. But I'll tell you this much—I was ready to fish some more, encouraged by this close encounter.

Keep Fishing

That's how sharing the gospel is. Some days you may get a big bite and almost "reel one in"! Other days you may not get anything close to a bite. So you just keep casting out your line and reeling it in. And you do it again and again.

To borrow another analogy concerning evangelism, there is "a time to sow and a time to reap." Paul explains the process very clearly in 1 Corinthians 3:6-8: "I planted the seed, Apollos watered it, but God made it grow. So neither he who plants nor he who waters is anything, but only God, who makes things grow. The man who plants and the man who waters have one purpose, and each will be rewarded according to his own labor" (NIV).

In the book of Ecclesiastes, we read, "He has made everything beautiful in its time" (Ecclesiastes 3:11). We also find, "The end of a thing is better than its beginning; the patient in spirit is better than the proud in spirit" (Ecclesiastes 7:8).

Be Patient

I don't know about you, but by nature, I am not a patient person. If I am driving on the freeway and one lane is moving slightly faster than another, I'm the guy weaving in and out of the lanes, wanting to get wherever I'm going just a little bit faster. When I go to the supermarket, I will carefully survey which line is the longest before I commit. And when I get in that "ten items or less" aisle, am I the only person who actually counts the items in the other people's carts to see if they fall within in the allotted amount? "Excuse me, but this man has eleven items! Please stop him now!"

When I go to pick up pizza and bring it home for my family, I cannot resist the temptation to have at least two pieces before I arrive at our house. And I can tell you that I have scorched the roof of my mouth more than once with the burning cheese of a pizza that needed to cool down first.

For that reason, when God tells me that I need to be patient when it comes to sharing my faith, it is not an easy task. Just as a fisherman often must sit quietly in his boat for hours at a time patiently awaiting a bite, so we "fishermen of souls" must be patient. We may not catch anything on a particular day, but we go back again, and we are patient with those to whom we share. It is important to remember that the "final answer" may not come at the end of a church service or a conversation with someone. We have heard so many stories over the years of those who have attended our Harvest Crusades and did not commit their lives to Christ at the actual crusade but came to the Lord later. Sometimes it is no later than when they step out into the stadium parking lot after the meeting. At other times it may be a day, a week, or a few months or even years later.

Fishermen are patient, and so are farmers. Consider a farmer planting his field. Seed is sown, but it germinates at different times. So when we share the gospel message with others. The "seed" was sown—

but it does not always germinate in some people as quickly as it does in others. Sometimes a seed sown today may not break ground until later. I remember hearing one story of a father and son who were out in downtown Waikiki handing out evangelistic flyers for our Harvest Crusade. The little boy asked his dad if he could give one of the flyers to a rather burly, menacing-looking, tattooed, body-pierced man. The dad somewhat reluctantly agreed, keeping a close watch on his son. The little boy cautiously approached this big, muscular fellow and timidly gave him the flyer. This big guy promptly snatched the flier and sort of wadded it up in his hand. From all appearances, it seemed to have been a rather unsuccessful encounter.

But things are not always as they seem.

That evening when the invitation to come to Christ was given at the crusade, that little boy and his father were waiting on the field as counselors to welcome those coming forward.

One of the first was that burly guy from Waikiki, coming to receive Christ!

Sometimes the seeds we sow today may not break ground for months, years, even decades. I have preached at many funeral services where people who had been witnessed to previously by the deceased finally made a decision to follow Christ. Some of these people had heard the gospel message for years—but it wasn't until the person who had shared with them had gone on to be with the Lord that they were ready to commit their lives to him.

So be patient. Be willing to wait. You may have such a burden for the lost that this is extremely difficult. But trust God, cast your line, and then be patient. After all, God needs to hook the fish!

4

KNOWING WHEN TO CAST

In the Right Place at the Right Time

A good fisherman instinctively knows where and when to cast his line or drop his nets. The same is true of sharing our faith. We must be sensitive to the timing and leading of the Holy Spirit. As Scripture reminds us, we must "be ready in season and out of season" (2 Timothy 4:2). This could also be translated, "Be on duty at all times." We need to be ready when it comes to telling others about the Lord.

I read the story of a fisherman named Larry Shaw, who was testing an outboard propeller on a lake in Ohio a few years ago. There, in a cove, he spotted a gigantic muskellunge fish near the surface. Shaw motored toward it and unsuccessfully cast out his line several times before the fish disappeared.

A half hour later, Shaw returned to the cove where he had first spotted the big muskie. It was back! Shaw turned on the electric trolling motor and headed toward the beast. As he crept closer, the massive fish suddenly started swimming toward the boat. Shaw quickly put on a leather glove and plunged his arm into the water, grabbing the fish behind the gills. That old fish started thrashing and twisting. Shaw was having trouble lifting the huge muskie into the boat. Fortunately, a nearby fisherman came over to help, and they were able to wrestle the monster into Shaw's boat. The muskellunge weighed over fifty-three pounds! If he had used a rod and reel, it probably would have broken the record for the biggest muskie ever caught in Ohio.

When asked about his fish, Shaw said, "I was at the right place at the right time, and I was fool enough to grab it."

That's the same attitude we should have in fishing for men. Being at the right place at the right time—and being "fool enough" to take a risk—to share the gospel.

Philip: The Prototype Evangelist

In the book of Acts, we read the story of Philip, who was having a successful ministry of sharing the gospel down in Samaria when he was instructed by God to go to the desert (see Acts 8:26-38). No detailed blueprint. No mention of whom to look for and share with. Just a command to go. But when he arrived, he found the "big fish" that Jesus had waiting for him: the treasurer for the queen of Ethiopia—a man of great importance and wealth.

In spite of his prestigious position, this man was

empty and searching for the meaning of life. His search led him to Jerusalem, the spiritual capital of the world. Tragically, instead of finding the vibrant faith of days gone by, he found a cold, legalistic, dead religion that did not give him what he needed. But he did acquire one very valuable thing from his trip there: a copy of Isaiah's writing, which would have been in scroll form.

As Philip came alongside this man's chariot, he found the man reading aloud from this scroll. Talk about a divine setup! Because Philip was ready and willing, he had the opportunity to lead that man to Christ.

Trust God's Timing

Missionary George Smith may have thought his ministry was a failure. He had been in Africa only a short time when he was driven from the country, leaving behind only one convert: a poor woman. He died not long after that, while on his knees, praying for Africa.

Years later, a group of men stumbled onto the place where George Smith had prayed. They also found a copy of the Scriptures he had left behind in Africa. Then they met the one convert of Smith's ministry. She shared the gospel with them, and they believed. The result of their encounter with the Bible and Smith's one convert was far-reaching. One hundred years later, a mission agency discovered that more than thirteen thousand converts had emerged from the ministry that George Smith had originally begun.

Actually, the analogy of a seed taking root fits George Smith's story better than catching a fish. You obviously know when you have caught a fish, but there may be a seed of the gospel being shared that you have forgotten all about. Then one day that seed, much to the surprise of many, breaks ground. So, like missionary George Smith, we need to keep faithfully sowing the seed of the gospel—because it's not over till God has finished working.

So you fish, you plant seeds, and you trust God to work. As you are sensitive to God's leading, he'll put you in the right place at the right time. As with Philip, he'll send you to the person who needs you. As with George Smith, you may not understand the timing or see the results, but you will have accomplished God's will. And that's really what it's all about!

5

BUILDING THE SKILLS

Know God's Word

It is important that a good fisherman have the right technique. A fisherman knows his equipment: lures, hooks, floats, weights, poles, bait, etc. Likewise, as we "fish" for men and women in this sea of life, we must use the appropriate tools: the Word of God and the leading of the Spirit.

This is why we must commit portions of Scripture to memory. Returning to Philip, as that high-ranking official from Ethiopia was reading aloud from the Scriptures, he asked Philip, "Of whom does the prophet say this, of himself or of some other man?" (Acts 8:34).

Philip, the seasoned "fisher of men," knew his tools (in this case, God's Word), and he was able to pull out the right hook and reel that big fish in! He did not falter in his reply. He knew his tools and used them well.

The use of Scripture is so important for so many reasons. For one, God promises that it will not return to him void: "The rain and snow come down from the heavens and stay on the ground to water the earth. They cause the grain to grow, producing seed for the farmer and bread for the hungry. It is the same with my word. I send it out, and it always produces fruit. It will accomplish all I want it to, and it will prosper everywhere I send it" (Isaiah 55:10-11, NLT).

You see, my word will return void. So will yours. But God's Word never will. That being said, let me add a couple of important thoughts here so that we can understand the balance. While it is essential to quote Scripture, that does not mean it has to be only in King James English (which often needs to be updated to be understood in our culture). Nor do you have to get a glazed look on your face as you quote it—or yell when you quote it. (These are all things I have seen well-meaning, but ineffective, Christians do.) Nor do you have to carry a fifteen-pound family Bible. You can quote the Bible conversationally, lovingly, and in a friendly manner. This is why it is so helpful to commit large portions of Scripture to memory.

While it is good to have a copy of the Word in your briefcase or your purse, the best place to carry the Word of God is in your heart! The psalmist writes, "Your word I have hidden in my heart, that I might not sin against You" (Psalm 119:11).

Paul reminds us of the importance of doing this carefully and accurately. Instructing young Timothy, Paul says, "Be diligent to present yourself approved to

God, a worker who does not need to be ashamed, rightly dividing the word of truth" (2 Timothy 2:15).

That phrase *rightly dividing* could also be translated "cutting it straight." It was a reference to the exactness demanded by such trades as carpentry, masonry, as well as Paul's trade of tentmaking. It conveys the idea of correctly and accurately using Scripture.

It's exciting when someone asks you a question and you draw a complete blank, and then suddenly an appropriate Scripture (that you have taken the time to commit to memory) just pops into your mind, and you share it with that person. What you are sharing is so good, you want to take notes on yourself!

You would not want to go into battle without knowing how your weapons worked. Nor would you want to build a house without knowing how your tools worked (especially your power tools!). And, of course, you could not catch many fish without knowing how to effectively use your rod, hooks, lures, and bait.

So know your Bible. This doesn't mean that you can't share until you've got whole books memorized or until you think you finally understand *everything* there is to know (none of us would ever be able to share our faith then!). As you share, however, keep learning, keep reading. If someone stumps you with a question, say that you'll go and find out. Learn how to find answers in God's Word. Work on memorizing. Those tools will be invaluable as you continue to share your faith in the sea of life.

6

TEAMWORK TO BRING IN THE CATCH

Know How to Work with Others

When you are fishing and a fish is hooked, a friend should be standing by to net it—just like that other fisherman in Ohio who helped Larry Shaw bag his fifty-three-pound muskie. It's teamwork! Cooperation is a key to effectively sharing your faith.

Did you ever notice that Jesus sent his disciples out in pairs? One could preach while another could pray. I remember how, as a young believer, I wanted to learn to be more effective in sharing the gospel. One day I went out with two more mature and experienced Christians (or so I thought). They approached some person, and one of them made a statement about Christ. Then the other Christian said that he did not really agree with that statement, and they began to argue with each other! The unbeliever was so disgusted with them that he just walked away while these two debated some fine point of theology. Obviously, we don't want to do that.

Working as a team can be such a blessing because the person you are speaking to about Christ may ask you a question you can't answer, but your partner can (or vice versa). Perhaps more important, while one is speaking, the other can be praying. Without question, sharing the gospel is a spiritual battle, and we all have a part to play. Scripture says, "Neither he who plants is anything, nor he who waters, but God who gives the increase" (1 Corinthians 3:7).

A classic example of believers working together is the Gospel story of the four men who brought their crippled friend to Jesus (see Luke 5:17-26). The house in which the Lord was ministering was jammed with people, and they could not get in. But these faithful friends would not be deterred. They decided to lower their friend down in front of the Lord—through the roof! So they climbed up there with their makeshift gurney on ropes and began to dig their way through the tiled roof of the home where Jesus was speaking.

Imagine the scene if you will. There is Jesus in this dark little room, opening the truths of the kingdom of God, when suddenly clumps of dirt and pieces of tile fall to the floor.

Dust starts dropping down, and a shaft of bright light bursts into the room. Then, down through a hole in the ceiling comes this crippled man, lying on his cot. He is slowly lowered until he lands right in front of Jesus.

You could understand if the Lord had been irritated by this interruption of his talk. Instead, Jesus was touched by this wonderful demonstration of faith in action, and he not only healed the man but forgave him of his sins as well.

You see, only one of those men working alone could not have presented his friend to Jesus like that. It would have been very difficult for two—even three. But when all four friends worked together, it resulted in a changed life.

Of course, there will be times when you're all on your own talking with a friend about your faith. But in a sense, you're not alone, because you will have (should have!) asked your believing friends to be praying for you. Then, when you can bring other believers into the picture to also be this person's friends or to answer this person's questions, you're using teamwork to help "catch another fish."

7

BAITING THE HOOK

Know How to Bait the Hook

Today there are all types of sophisticated devices that harness the latest technology to detect schools of fish, utilizing radar, electronics, and depth finders. I heard about a special camera that an angler can now use to take a peek under the water and see where the fish are. Then there are thousands of lures you can choose from.

When we go fishing for men, we need to realize that what works for one does not necessarily work for another. Don't get me wrong. I am not suggesting that the essential gospel is not the same for every person, for indeed it is. The bottom line, as I will point out later, is that very message. At the same time, however, we may initially approach different people with different "bait" to get their attention.

Different Bait for Different Fish

For instance, if someone is strung out on drugs and/or alcohol, you might emphasize that only Jesus can fill the void that person has tried to fill with these substances. If you once struggled with these yourself, you could share your own personal story of how God filled the void in your life you once tried to fill with these cheap worldly imitations. If it is not your personal experience, you could mention the stories of some you probably know personally who came out of this kind of background and are now walking with the Lord.

If you are speaking to a person who is terminally ill or is on his or her deathbed, obviously the most important thing to that person is not so much filling a void in his or her life but preparing for eternity. You could share the great promises of Scripture concerning life beyond the grave when we put our complete faith and trust in Jesus Christ. And if you come upon a person who has gone from relationship to relationship, trying to fill a void for God with a man or a woman, you could speak of what it is to have a relationship with the living God who will never abandon or "dump" him or her.

Some people may offer a quick statement about the Lord to practically everyone they meet. That can be good to some degree, but it is far more effective to take the time to share the gospel with one person. Like Jesus, we need to recognize the specific needs of individuals. God wants us to be responsible "sharp-shooters," not haphazard "machine gunners"!

You may not have noticed this yet, but the favorite subject of conversation for most people is themselves.

That is why I have found one of the best ways to share one's faith is to simply listen. That's right—listen.

You could compare this type of evangelism to a visit to the doctor's office. The doctor starts by saying something like, "Tell me where it's hurting." He does this so he can make a proper diagnosis. Then, after carefully listening to the description of your pain or ailment, he will prescribe the appropriate medication or procedure.

In the same way, one of the best ways to begin sharing Christ with others is to ask them about themselves. Find out about their family and background. Ask them what their thoughts are on a number of subjects. When a person shares his or her ideas, however, you don't want to immediately start disagreeing with him or her. Saying something like, "You actually believe something as stupid as that?" "What an idiot!" or "Wrong again, Philistine!" will only put that person on the defensive.

Just listen. Take it in. Then your turn will come. Try to build a bridge from a statement that that person has made. For all practical purposes, this is what Jesus did when he conversed with (not just spoke to) the woman at the well. He asked her questions. He drew her out. He listened. He responded. And a conversion took place that day, as you'll see in the next chapter.

8

COMMUNICATION IS CRITICAL

Jesus, the Master Communicator

Jesus never dealt with any two people in exactly the same way. He varied his approach from person to person. He was, after all, the Master Communicator. Central in his dealings with others was his compassion.

This is especially seen in Jesus' encounter with the Samaritan woman at the well (John 4:3-42, NLT). Scripture says that in spite of his busy schedule and all that he had to do, he "had to go through Samaria," no doubt knowing that there was a lonely, hurting woman who would be coming to a certain well in that region. As he was waiting for her at the well, there she came, drawing water in the heat of the day. She was an outcast, known for her immoral life. She had gone from marriage to marriage, each one ending tragically in divorce. And when she met Jesus, she was living in an immoral relationship with a man.

If anyone had the right to get up on a soapbox and give her a strong sermon about sexual sin, it was Jesus! He knew everything about her. He could have addressed all of the sins that she had committed. But he didn't.

As they conversed a bit, she became somewhat flippant in her responses to him. Jesus could have retorted, "Repent, you adulteress!" Yet, it is interesting to note that he did not do that. He saw behind the facade to what was really troubling this woman. Instead of hammering her for her immoral lifestyle, he went to the root of her problem: she was empty and separated from God. Then, lovingly and tactfully, Jesus shared with her that he as God could fill the void in her life that she had previously tried to fill with men. He essentially told her that if she drank from the "well" of relationships, she would thirst again. But if she drank from his well of living water, she would never thirst again. She accepted Jesus that day, and immediately became a witness. Jesus stayed in that town for two days and many people believed—largely because this woman told them about Jesus.

How different Jesus' approach to that woman is from many well-meaning but poorly trained Christians today. They act as though they are robots, spouting the same clichés to each person they meet without recognizing each individual's need. It is important to know to whom you are speaking and how best to grab their attention.

Know Your Audience

This was the very strategy Paul used when he spoke to the people at Mars Hill in Athens (see Acts 17:16-34). Athens was the cultural and intellectual center of the world at that time. But as Paul walked the streets of this magnificent city with its incredible architecture and gleaming monuments, he was troubled. Everywhere he looked, there stood a statue, an altar, a temple, or a shrine to some god. They were made out of stone, brass, and even gold, silver, ivory, and marble—beautiful works of art, but idols nonetheless. The city was overrun with idols. In fact, it was said in that day that it was easier to find a god in Athens than a person.

Paul thought and prayed carefully about what he would say to these Athenians when he appeared before them. He could have understandably delivered a searing sermon on idolatry and false worship. But Paul saw what was behind it all. These people were largely ignorant. They really didn't know any better. So he stood before them and said, "Men of Athens, I notice that you are very religious, for as I was walking along I saw your many altars. And one of them had this inscription on it—'To an Unknown God.' You have been worshiping him without knowing who he is, and now I wish to tell you about him" (Acts 17:22-23, NLT).

What a perfect opening statement! Talk about building bridges. At that moment, I'm sure that the Athenians were really listening.

Avoid Arguments

Another practical tip: Don't be drawn into an argument. Scripture reminds us:

Don't have anything to do with foolish and stupid arguments, because you know they produce quarrels. And the Lord's servant must not quarrel; instead, he must be kind to everyone, able to teach, not resentful. Those who oppose him he must gently instruct, in the hope that God will grant them repentance leading them to a knowledge of the truth, and that they will come to their senses and escape from the trap of the devil, who has taken them captive to do his will. (2 Timothy 2:23-26, NIV)

The woman at the well tried to draw Jesus into an argument about the religious and cultural differences between Samaritans and Jews. Instead of entering into a fruitless discussion, Jesus brought her back to the main message.

No one has ever been argued into the kingdom of God. There is a place for disagreement and for clearly making your point. At the same time, however, we must be careful not to lose sight of our objective. The goal is not to win an argument, but to win a person to Christ.

Use Tact

We need to utilize something that is sorely lacking in the evangelism toolbox of many believers today. It is called tact. Tact is essentially putting yourself in the other person's shoes. It is an intuitive perception of what to say and when to say it. We do not need to unnecessarily alienate the person to whom we are speaking.

I read about a barber who, as a young Christian, attended a meeting one night where the speaker stressed the need to share the gospel with others. The barber knew he was lacking in this area, so he determined that he would speak to the first person who sat in his chair for a haircut the next day.

The next morning, after the customer had been seated and the apron was tucked around his neck, the barber began to strop his razor vigorously. Testing the edge, he turned to the man in the chair and blurted out, "Friend, are you ready to die and meet God?"

The man looked at the razor and fled out the door—apron and all! The barber had the right idea. He just needed to use a little tact.

Going back to Philip, that evangelist displayed his tact brilliantly as he shared the gospel with the searching man from Ethiopia. As that man read aloud from Isaiah's book, Philip came up alongside him and asked, "Do you understand what you are reading?" (Acts 8:30, NLT). Now that is friendly, bridge-building stuff. He didn't huff, "Hey, you! Yeah, you, you pagan! Did you know that you're going to hell?"

Instead, he sought to reach out to this man. And the Ethiopian responded in kind: "How can I [understand this], when there is no one to instruct me?" (Acts 8:31, NLT). Then he invited Philip into his chariot to do just that. The result, once again, was a conversion.

Paul summed it up this way:

> When I am with the Jews, I become one of them so that I can bring them to Christ. When I am with those who follow the Jewish laws, I do the same, even though I am not subject to the law, so that I can bring them to Christ. When I am with the Gentiles who do not have the Jewish law, I fit in with them as much as I can. In this way, I gain their confidence and bring them to Christ. . . . Yes, I try to find common ground with everyone so that I might bring them to Christ. I do all this to spread the Good News, and in doing so I enjoy its blessings. (1 Corinthians 9:20-23, NLT).

Pray for God to give you sensitivity to whomever you speak about your faith. If you know them well, key in on their needs. If you don't, be sensitive and listen. You'll learn what is keeping them from the faith, and what you might be able to say to help. Don't argue, be tactful. You'll listen, and then you'll find that they will listen to you as well.

9

A STORY WORTH TELLING

Tell Your Own Story

One of the best ways to "build a bridge" to someone who does not have a relationship with Christ is through your personal testimony. This is basically your story of how you came to Jesus Christ. The wonderful thing about your testimony is that even if you are relatively young in the faith, you can still share about what God has done for you personally.

Consider the blind man who was miraculously healed by Jesus. He was being cross-examined by the religious authorities on the fine points of theology when he gave this classic response: "One thing I do know. I was blind but now I see!" (John 9:25, NIV).

Let me tell you, that explanation is a lot more than most people in this world know today. Though a person may disagree with what you believe, they cannot deny what actually happened to you.

You can tell him or her of your life and attitude before coming to Christ, then explain the changes that came afterward. When an unbeliever sees that you can relate to his or her own life, he or she may be more open to what you have to say. In a way, it's like preaching directly to him or her without really doing so in so many words.

You might say something like, "I heard this Christian say that I needed to give my life to Christ. My first inclination was, 'I am a good person. I don't really need Jesus. That's for weak people.' But then that Christian said, . . ." and you could explain that person's response to your excuses. You see, in doing this, you are putting yourself in the other person's shoes.

No Story Like Yours

It is interesting to note how often the apostle Paul used his personal testimony when sharing the gospel. You would think that this man of brilliant intellect, trained in the great knowledge of his day and possessing a tremendous grasp and understanding of Scripture, would lean upon his extensive knowledge and oratorical skills when telling others of the gospel. Yet more often than not, when standing before Roman governors and leaders, Paul would begin by telling his personal story of how he came to know Jesus Christ as his Savior and Lord.

Every believer has a testimony. Granted, some may be more dramatic than others, yet there is someone out there who is just like you. I mentioned earlier that if you had personally struggled with something, such as drugs or alcohol, before you were a Christian, you could share that fact as you show how God can fill the void in your life that you had previously tried to fill with substances.

You may say, "But Greg, I did not come from a background like that at all. In fact, I've lived a relatively upright, moral life." Perhaps you tried to be as considerate and caring as possible. You were even somewhat religious. But there was still something missing in your life. One day, you discovered that "something" was someone. You needed Jesus, and you came to put your faith in him. You realized that no matter how good you were, you were not quite good enough!

Don't you realize that is a powerful testimony? It is just as valid as the story of someone who has come out of a life of crime, gangs, or drugs. It's just different. When you get down to the bottom line, we all essentially have the same testimony. We were all separated from God by sin. We all crossed that line deliberately and repeatedly. We all needed a Savior. Whether we were a down-and-outer or an up-and-outer, we were still out! But then Jesus came in.

Don't Exaggerate or Glorify the Past

Sometimes there is a temptation to exaggerate just how bad we were or make things sound a little bit worse than they were. Avoid that temptation. Always be truthful and honest when relating your story. I have heard some Christians share their personal testimonies, and they seem to get a bit more dramatic with each telling.

One other thing I would add about sharing your personal story: never focus on what you gave up for God but rather on what God gave up for you. For instance, some people will vividly describe the "old days" before they knew the Lord with such excitement and passion that it will sound like their old lives were better than their new ones. Or they may speak of the great sacrifices they made to follow Jesus. "I had it all in my old life," they may boast. "Women, parties, fun, success, money—you name it, I had it!" Then with a somber look on their faces and tears in their eyes, they intone, "But I am here to tell you I gave it all up for Jesus. Hallelujah!"

Oh, please. What did you really give up? You gave up emptiness, an ever-present guilt, a constant fear of death, and a certain judgment that was to follow. What did God give you in its place? He gave you fulfillment, forgiveness, and the hope of life beyond the grave.

Again, do not emphasize what you gave up for God but rather what he gave up for you. He sent his own dear Son to lay his life down for you at the cross of Calvary.

Make a Beeline to the Cross

I already mentioned how Paul often used his personal testimony of how he came to Christ. Still, he always made a "beeline to the cross." In other words, he always came back to the message of Jesus Christ's death and resurrection.

Paul wrote, "When I came to you, brothers, I did not come with eloquence or superior wisdom as I proclaimed to you the testimony about God. For I resolved to know nothing while I was with you except Jesus Christ and him crucified" (1 Corinthians 2:1-2, NIV).

What exactly is this gospel message we are to proclaim to this lost world? Paul gives a simple summation of the gospel in 1 Corinthians 15:1-4:

> Now, brothers, I want to remind you of the gospel I preached to you, which you received and on which you have taken your stand. By this gospel you are saved, if you hold firmly to the word I preached to you. Otherwise, you have believed in vain. For what I received I passed on to you as of first importance: that Christ died for our sins according to the Scriptures, that he was buried, that he was raised on the third day according to the Scriptures. (NIV)

Embed that thought deep into your mind. The gospel in a nutshell is that Christ died for our sins, was buried, and was raised on the third day. There are other elements I could mention, but that is the cornerstone—the death and resurrection of Jesus Christ. Someone once asked C. H. Spurgeon if he could summarize his Christian faith in a few words. He replied, "It is all in four words: Jesus died for me."

An Embarrassing Personal Experience

I had an experience as a very young Christian that showed me early on the importance of knowing the Scriptures, for I was unprepared and, as a result, shamed.

The incident took place not long after I had the privilege of leading to the Lord that lady I mentioned at the beginning of this book. I was out on the streets of Newport Beach looking for more people to share the gospel with. Allow me to backtrack for a moment. I had a friend I had known since early childhood named Gregg. Soon after I had accepted the Lord into my life, I ran into Gregg and told him of my decision. Seeing the look of concern on his face, I reassured him by saying, "Don't worry now, Gregg. I am not going to become one of those religious fanatics walking around with a Bible and a cross around my neck, saying, 'Praise the Lord!' I'm going to do this on my terms."

Gregg seemed satisfied with my reassurance. I had not seen him for a couple of weeks, and my passion for sharing the gospel had grown quite a bit after leading that lady to Christ. As I was walking down the street in Newport Beach, whom do I see walking toward me but Gregg. In my hand was a Bible, and around my neck—you guessed it—was a cross. Before I could catch myself, I blurted out to Gregg, "Praise the Lord!"

We both had a good laugh. He could not believe his eyes. I said, "Gregg, I know this looks crazy, but because Jesus is so real and has changed my life so much, I'm out here on the beach, telling people about him!"

He was listening.

I thought to myself, *What if my friend Gregg became a Christian?* So I began to share with him what Christ said and how to know him.

He seemed interested.

I continued on, excited with the possibility of his coming to Christ, when suddenly someone interrupted us. It was some guy who had been eavesdropping on our conversation.

"So you're a Christian?" he barked.

I eagerly said I was.

"Well, Christian," he challenged, "I have a few questions for you!"

I thought to myself, *Fire away! I'm already two weeks old in the Lord. I'm ready for anything!*

Then this fellow fired off about four or five hard questions in rapid succession—and I didn't have a clue about how to answer them.

Gregg joined in, "Yeah, Laurie. What about all that?"

I was speechless and embarrassed. "I really don't know the answers, guys," I said sheepishly. They both walked away, and I felt as though I had failed God. But that experience was a watershed of sorts for me. It made me search the Scriptures. The Bible tells us in 1 Peter 3:15, "Always be ready to give a defense to everyone who asks you a reason for the hope that is in you, with meekness and fear."

There was nothing wrong with my not knowing those answers—even people who have been believers for many years still don't have answers to some questions, because some things just require faith. However, I needed to be willing to answer these guys with a confident "I don't know, but I'll find out for you." They were trying to divert me—and I let them do it. That day, I learned that I needed to prepare myself for those kinds of situations. And you should do the same. As you prepare and practice, you will develop the skill of seeing through the diversions and getting back to your story of what Jesus did for you—the story that only you can tell.

10

THE CORNERSTONES
OF THE GOSPEL

What Exactly Is the Gospel?

The gospel!

We hear that phrase tossed around a lot today. We call a certain style of music "gospel music," designated as such because of a certain sound it has. When we really want someone to believe what we are saying, we might add, "Listen—this is the 'gospel truth'!" But sadly, the word *gospel* has largely lost its meaning in today's culture.

It is my personal opinion that most Americans—much less the rest of the world—have not really heard the gospel. We hear some people say that they are "preaching the gospel," when in reality they don't even seem to know what that term really means. For that matter, I think there may be a surprising number of people in the church itself who do not actually know what the gospel message really is. According to one survey, 75 percent do not even know what John 3:16 says!

What is the gospel? What elements must be in it for it to be accurate? Are there false gospels we must be aware of? You might say, "I'll leave that to you preachers and theologians to figure out. All I know is I'm already saved and going to heaven!"

But wait! We all need to know what the gospel is for two very important reasons: (1) We want to make sure that we have heard the true gospel and have responded to it, lest we have a false hope concerning a salvation we *think* we have; and (2) Jesus told us to "go into all the world and preach the gospel" (Mark 16:15)!

Those words are not merely addressed to pastors, teachers, evangelists, and missionaries; they are addressed to every follower of Jesus Christ! We cannot be disengaged or disinterested in this subject, for people's eternal destinies literally hang in the balance.

What would you think of a surgeon who just started cutting away at a patient without really knowing what he was doing? One mistake, and that person could be disabled for life or could even die on the operating table. Yet this message we bring has even more far-reaching consequences than that—for there are eternal ramifications. Still, so many are sloppy in this area.

Good News, Bad News

What elements must be present for the gospel to be the gospel? A technical definition of the word *gospel* is "good news." We've all heard the expression "I have some good news and some bad news." Upon hearing a statement like that, we usually want to know the worst first.

You may have heard about the doctor who said to his patient, "I have some good news and some bad news."

The patient replied, "What is the good news?"

The doctor said, "You only have three weeks to live."

Exasperated, the patient replied, "If that's the good news, what's the bad news?"

The doctor answered, "I should have told you two weeks ago."

When it comes to the gospel, the bad news is the fact that we all stand as sinners before a holy God. No matter who we are, we have all sinned—sometimes in ignorance but more often on purpose. Yet even as a jeweler will display a beautiful ring or necklace against a dark velvet background to accentuate its beauty, God has chosen to show us just how good the Good News is by first telling us the bad news.

Once we see our complete weakness, our inability to do anything whatsoever to alleviate our wretched condition, we can better appreciate the ultimate gift God has given us: "When we were still without strength, in due time Christ died for the ungodly. For scarcely for a righteous man will one die; yet perhaps for a good man someone would even dare to die. But

God demonstrates His own love toward us, in that while we were still sinners, Christ died for us" (Romans 5:6-8).

Ponder that a moment. Consider the beauty of salvation against the dark background of our sin. God didn't give us this gift because we in any way deserved it; he gave it to us because we were so undeserving. There was no other way to satisfy the righteous demands of God; we were utterly incapable of improving ourselves (much less save ourselves), and we faced a future in hell because of our sin. Yet God, in his great love, sent his own Son to come down from heaven and die on the cross in our place. I love the way Paul personalized it when he said, "Christ . . . loved me and gave Himself for me" (Galatians 2:20).

A Gap Only God Could Bridge

There was no other way to resolve this serious sin issue we all face. We know that God is perfect. And we know that man is imperfect and sinful. So Jesus, the God-man, was uniquely qualified to bridge the gap between sinful humanity and a holy God. He was the only one who could ever do that: "All this is from God, who reconciled us to himself through Christ and gave us the ministry of reconciliation: that God was reconciling the world to himself in Christ, not counting men's sins against them. And he has committed to us the message of reconciliation" (2 Corinthians 5:18-19, NIV).

It is not about what I did to please or reach God. I did everything to displease and fail to reach him. As this passage says, "All this is from God, who reconciled us to himself through Christ." This is why Jesus Christ is the only way to the Father! In fact, he said so himself in John 14:6: "I am the way, the truth, and the life. No one comes to the Father except through Me."

In the times in which we are living, it is tempting to soft-pedal this issue and say something along the lines of "We all worship the same God. You can choose your path. I've chosen mine. Mine is Christ. But if you want to worship some other way, that's fine." It's *not* fine!

The apostle Peter underscores this important fact, echoing Christ's words: "There is salvation in no one else! There is no other name in all of heaven for people to call on to save them" (Acts 4:12, NLT).

Paul said the same thing: "There is one God and one Mediator between God and men, the Man Christ Jesus" (1 Timothy 2:5). Jesus, being God, was the only one who could bridge the gap and shed his blood in our place. For we as Christians to say anything else is not only wrong—it is a misrepresentation of the gospel!

There, on that cross, all the sin of the world was poured upon Jesus Christ as he became the sin sacrifice for us: "He made Him who knew no sin to be sin for us, that we might become the righteousness of God in Him" (2 Corinthians 5:21). If humankind could have reached God any other way, Jesus would not have had to die. His voluntary death on the cross clearly illustrates the fact that there is no other way. Those who reject his loving offer of forgiveness—which is extended to all—do so at their own peril.

It's a Done Deal

That is why Jesus cried out these three words on the cross of Calvary: "It is finished" (John 19:30). That phrase can be translated many ways: "It is made an end of; it is paid; it is performed; it is accomplished!"

What was made an end of? Our sins—and the guilt that accompanied them.

What was paid? The price of redemption!

What was performed? The righteous requirements of the law!

What was accomplished? The work the Father had given Jesus to do.

Finished was Satan's stronghold on humanity: "[Jesus] . . . wiped out the handwriting of requirements that was against us, which was contrary to us. And He has taken it out of the way, having nailed it to the cross. Having disarmed principalities and powers, He made a public spectacle of them, triumphing over them in it" (Colossians 2:14-15).

Simple, but Powerful

In the book of Romans, Paul refers to the explosive power of the gospel: "I am not ashamed of the gospel of

Christ, for it is the power of God to salvation for everyone who believes" (Romans 1:16). That is a profound statement coming from such an intelligent, gifted communicator as Paul. If anyone could have talked people into becoming Christians by mere mental skills, it would have been Paul. Yet it is amazing to read the accounts in the book of Acts as he stood before government leaders, the rich, and the powerful and shared the simple message of Jesus' dying on the cross.

Paul is reminding us that there is power in the simple message of the life, words, death, and resurrection of Jesus Christ. We often underestimate the raw power the gospel has in reaching even the most hardened heart. Don't underestimate its appeal. Don't be ashamed of its simplicity. Don't add to it or take away from it. Just proclaim it—then stand back and watch what God will do.

I have been amazed time and time again at how God so powerfully uses this simple yet incredibly profound message to radically change lives. I have seen it transform hardened satanists as well as devoutly religious people who had previously not understood their need for Christ. I have witnessed its ability to heal broken families, break people's addictions to drugs, and free individuals who have been deceived by various cults.

The gospel of Christ is the most powerful message ever given, and through it God can and does change even the most broken of lives.

11

BEWARE OF IMITATIONS

What the Gospel Is Not

1. Beware of a watered-down gospel that has no "teeth."

To "water down" the gospel means to speak of God's forgiveness without any mention of repentance or to present Jesus Christ as though he were some mere "additive" to make one's life a little better. It would be like saying, "All you have to do is ask him in, and your life will be better, your clothes cleaner, and your teeth whiter!" This is obviously an exaggeration, but it is not too far from what some people are saying as you might think. We must not leave out the important aspects of repentance and obedience. I have already pointed out that we can appeal to the emptiness and voids in people's lives, especially as we begin our time of sharing the gospel with them. At the same time, however, we must get down to brass tacks.

2. Beware of a rule-laden or overly complex gospel that strips the message of its simplicity and power.

This would involve telling people that first they have

to be baptized before they can become Christians, or that they must dress a certain way to be forgiven, etc. This is essentially adding works to a salvation that Scripture reminds us is "a gift from God" and is not "a reward for the good things we have done" (Ephesians 2:8-9, NLT). Again, this is why Scripture reminds us that we as Christians should be "rightly dividing the word of truth" (2 Timothy 2:15). So read this section very carefully. As Scripture advises us, "Watch your life and doctrine closely. Persevere in them, because if you do, you will save both yourself and your hearers" (1 Timothy 4:16, NIV).

We must know what the Bible teaches. We must know what we believe. We must be careful to present the gospel accurately, making sure that certain key elements are in place. Why? Because there is a counterfeit gospel out there.

Beware of a False Gospel

Make no mistake about it. The devil is a master manipulator and imitator. One of the greatest tactics he has used with tremendous effect over the centuries is to imitate something—to offer a counterfeit version of it that is close enough to be believable to some but far enough away from the truth to actually damage the person who believes it.

There is a false or counterfeit gospel. Paul writes to the Galatians:

I am astonished that you are so quickly deserting the one who called you by the grace of Christ and are turning to a different gospel— which is really no gospel at all. Evidently some people are throwing you into confusion and are trying to pervert the gospel of Christ. But even if we or an angel from heaven should preach a gospel other than the one we preached to you, let him be eternally condemned! (Galatians 1:6-8, NIV)

Today, there are many new TV programs and movies coming out of Hollywood that deal with spiritual themes. They underscore such things as faith, life after death, the meaning of life, and more. The problem that I have observed with most of them is that their message is lopsided. It's a "Hollywood feel-good" belief that could potentially give a person false assurance.

I recently watched a TV program along these lines that emphasized the theme "God is love." While that certainly is a biblical and important message (one that I repeatedly emphasize myself), we do not want to lose sight of the fact that this God of love is also a God of justice, holiness, and perfection. Moreover, we don't want to forget to point out that God showed this love to us by sending his only Son to die on the cross for our sins. And the only way to come to know this God of love is through Christ.

This "false gospel" Paul warns us against says that all we have to do is believe—but it doesn't say that we need to repent. It speaks of heaven but leaves out the message of hell. On the other hand, it can be so complex that no one can unravel it, or it can come laden with rules and regulations that one must keep to find forgiveness. That's not very "good news."

General William Booth, founder of the Salvation Army, wrote of the dangers he saw that faced the message of the gospel in the twentieth century (and, I might add, the twenty-first century, too). Among other things, he saw a "gospel" that would present:

- Christianity without Christ
- Forgiveness without repentance
- Salvation without regeneration
- Heaven without hell

While this watered-down gospel is a real problem, so also is a gospel that would only warn of judgment and not offer God's gracious forgiveness.

This is another important reason for you to know God's Word. Ask God to guide you as you study. Pray for discernment in order to know a false gospel when you hear it. Be ready with the truth. People are longing for it!

12

THE STEPS TO THE DECISION

Reeling in the Fish

Suppose that the person you have been sharing the gospel with seems ready to receive Christ. You ask, "Is there any good reason why you should not accept Jesus Christ right now?"

Much to your shock, they say, "No. I want to accept Christ right now!" What then? I like to make sure that person fully understands what he or she is doing. I often make five points at the end of my evangelistic messages. They were adapted from a message by Billy Graham at Madison Square Garden in the fifties. Here they are:

1. Realize that you are a sinner.
This is a hard one for people to admit. Yet Romans 3:23 clearly says, "All have sinned and fall short of the glory of God." We must first accept full responsibility for our sins.

2. Recognize that Jesus Christ died for your sin.
Because there was no other way to resolve this problem of our sin, God sent his own Son to die in our

place on the cross of Calvary. Romans 5:8 says, "While we were still sinners, Christ died for us." Jesus said, "God so loved the world that He gave His only begotten Son, that whoever believes in Him should not perish but have everlasting life" (John 3:16).

3. You must repent.

Acts 17:30 says, "God . . . commands all people everywhere to repent" (NIV). To *repent* means that you have been going the wrong way in life, and you need to start going God's way. Instead of running from God, you run *to* him.

4. You must receive Jesus Christ into your life.

Jesus said, "Behold, I stand at the door and knock. If anyone hears My voice and opens the door, I will come in" (Revelation 3:20). Being a Christian is not merely believing a creed or even going to a church. You can do those things and not necessarily have your sin forgiven and have Christ in your heart. There must come a moment in every person's life where he or she says, "Lord, come in." Scripture tells us, "To all who believed him and accepted him, he gave the right to become children of God" (John 1:12, NLT).

5. You must do it now!

Second Corinthians 6:2 says, "Today is the day of salvation" (NLT). This could be the person's last opportunity to respond to the gospel.

13

A Decision Deferred
Is No Decision

Seize the Moment!

Let's say that the person you have been sharing with is ready right then and there to make that commitment. Then I strongly urge you, if possible, to find a quiet place and to lead the person in a prayer of receiving Christ. Don't tell him or her to think it over and get back to you. Seize the moment!

Why is it so important to do it right then? The story is told of the great evangelist, D. L. Moody, who preached an evangelistic message one night in Chicago. He decided to give his listeners a night to think over the question "What will you do with Jesus?" Then he asked them to consider coming back the next evening to hear him preach again.

The next morning Chicago lay in ashes. On October 8, 1871, the very night of his message, the Great Chicago Fire started. Many who were in his audience died in that blaze. To his dying day, Moody regretted that he had told the people to wait. He never forgot that hard-learned lesson. He later wrote:

I have never dared to give an audience a week to think of their salvation since. If they were lost they would rise up in judgment against me. I want to tell one lesson I learned that night which I have never forgotten, and that is when I preach, to press Christ upon the people then and there, and try to bring them to a decision on the spot. I would rather have my right hand cut off than to give an audience a week now to decide what to do with Jesus.

14

The Reasons People Say No

Why People Don't Come to Christ

Many of us know what it is like to be sharing the gospel with someone and suddenly find ourselves barraged by an endless stream of questions and so-called "reasons" as to why the person has not trusted Christ as Savior.

I believe that most of these are not honest questions or reasons as much as they are excuses. And you know what an excuse is, don't you? It is just a fancy lie.

Excuses have been defined as "the skin of a reason stuffed with a lie." An excuse is what we offer up when we really don't want to do something. Many will hide behind excuses because they really don't want to come to Christ. And the reason they don't want to come to Christ is that they really do not want to change. I will give you the primary reason people do not come to Christ in the next chapter. (You can skip ahead if you want.) Let me first address four of the most commonly asked questions about the Christian faith:

1. If God is so good and loving, why does he allow evil?
2. How can you Christians say that Jesus is the only way? Don't all roads lead ultimately to God?
3. How can a God of love send people to hell?
4. The reason I am not a Christian is because there are so many hypocrites!

1. If God is so good and loving, why does he allow evil?
This one is always on the top of people's lists of questions about God! We are asked, "Why does he allow babies to be born blind, or war, or injustice, or tragedy?" In the classic statement of the problem, either God is all-powerful but not all good; therefore, he *does not* stop evil. Or he is all good but not all-powerful; therefore, he *can't* stop evil.

The general tendency is to blame God for evil and suffering, passing all responsibility on to him. However, God is getting a bad rap! You see, people were created with the ability to choose. We have the freedom to choose to love or not to love, to do right or to do wrong, to obey or disobey. In the Garden of Eden, those first people made the wrong choice, and sin entered into the world: "Sin entered the world through one man, and death through sin, and in this way death came to all men, because all sinned" (Romans 5:12, NIV).

As a result, we live in a world that is fallen and imperfect. Because sin entered the world through Adam, the entire planet has been affected. The curse came not only on humanity, but on all creation as well. The repercussion of that was the entrance of sin into the world. And with that sin came many problems, like sickness and even death. Up to that point, men and women would have lived forever in their perfect bodies. But now this body of ours wears out and breaks down with the passing of time. Disease, sickness, disabilities—all came as a result of the curse of sin. They are not a punishment for a sin that we have committed, but rather are the result of sin in general.

The point that we must keep in mind is that *man*—not God—is responsible for sin! Take wars, for instance. They are not initiated by God, but by humanity. James tells us where they come from: "What is causing the quarrels [wars] and fights among you? Isn't it the whole army of evil desires at war within you? You want what you don't have, so you scheme and kill to get it. You are jealous for what others have, and you can't possess it, so you fight and quarrel to take it away from them" (James 4:1-2, NLT).

Yet, in spite of our wrong choices, God intervenes. He is able and willing to forgive us, even when we have horribly sinned. The Bible says, "If we confess our sins, He is faithful and just to forgive us our sins and to cleanse us from all unrighteousness" (1 John 1:9). God can even use something like sickness to bring us to himself. God can speak to us through tragedy or

71

hardship. C. S. Lewis wrote, "God whispers to us in our pleasures, speaks in our conscience, but shouts in our pains; it is his megaphone to arouse a deaf world." Sadly, God has to use his "megaphone" for some of us. It's the only thing that will get our attention. The psalmist writes, "Before I was afflicted I went astray, but now I keep Your word" (Psalm 119:67).

As Christians, however, we have the hope that one day "God will wipe away every tear from their eyes; there shall be no more death, nor sorrow, nor crying. There shall be no more pain, for the former things have passed away" (Revelation 21:4). You can point out to the person asking this question that only Christians have that hope. Then ask him or her, "Do you?"

2. How can you Christians say that Jesus is the only way? Don't all roads lead ultimately to God?

I touched on this objection briefly in the section relating to the basic gospel message. This particular cornerstone of the Christian faith is especially irritating to many unbelievers. They may get in your face and shout, "Are you saying that Jesus Christ is the only way and that if someone does not believe in him, they are actually going to hell?" Then they proceed to label you as "narrow," "bigoted," "insensitive," and (probably the worst thing that you can be accused of in this day and age) "intolerant."

To such people, it may sound as though you are implying that you are somehow better than they are or that you look down on them because of your belief in Christ. Yet you need to let them know that the reason you believe that Jesus Christ is the only way to the Father is quite simply because he said so himself. As I quoted earlier, Jesus tells us in Scripture, "I am the way, the truth, and the life. No one comes to the Father except through Me" (John 14:6). If I claim to be his follower and believe his words, then I would be less than honest if I said anything but this.

As a Christian, I am not better than or superior to anyone else. I am just one beggar telling another beggar where to find food. Someone may say, "If a person is really sincere in what he or she believes, he or she will get to heaven." This type of fuzzy, illogical thinking is typical of so many today, causing them to make the most important decisions of life on the basis of their personal thoughts and feelings. It is as though they were somehow the "moral center of the universe."

Do you really think sincerity is enough? Take this line of reasoning to its logical conclusion. If a person truly is sincere in what he or she believes and tries to live a good life, then he or she will get to heaven. So Adolf Hitler is in heaven, right? He sincerely believed that what he was doing was right. Charles Manson is OK, too, right? And what about Jim Jones?

The person may protest, "No! They were not good!" But according to whose definition? Yours? Mine? The person's next door? Is it determined by consensus? Why is it wrong to lie, steal, and murder? Who says? It comes back to the fact that we have to have a set of absolutes we live by. We cannot simply make up the rules as we go. Many want to believe that all roads lead to God and that every religion is basically true. We would like to think that all religions blend beautifully together, but they really do not. You see, only Jesus Christ was both God and man. Only Jesus was qualified to bridge the way to a holy God. The Bible says, "There is one God and one Mediator between God and men, the Man Christ Jesus" (1 Timothy 2:5). Jesus also said, "He who is not with Me is against Me" (Luke 11:23). Jesus does not say, "Admire me." He says, "Follow me!"

And that is the decision each person must make.

3. How can a God of love send people to hell?

God doesn't send anyone to hell. People send themselves there. Hell was never created for people, it was created for the devil and his angels. When speaking of the destiny of those who hypocritically claimed to follow him, Jesus said, "Depart from Me, you cursed, into the everlasting fire *prepared for the devil and his angels*" (Matthew 25:41, italics mine). God doesn't want anyone to go to hell! In Ezekiel 33:11, God says, "I have no pleasure in the death of the wicked, but that the wicked turn from his way and live." Second Peter 3:9 reminds us, "The Lord is not . . . willing that any should perish, but that all should come to repentance."

Here's an illustration you could use in explaining this to an unbeliever. Let's say that you are driving on the freeway and are on your way to cross a large bridge over a raging river. Suddenly, you see a large sign that reads: *Warning! Bridge Out! Use Other Exit!* Nevertheless, you are determined, so you speed up toward that bridge. As you get closer, you see more signs: *Do Not Enter! Danger! Bridge Out!* Still, you frantically speed on. As you get really close, you see police cars with lights flashing and officers waving and yelling for you to turn back. Yet you continue on until you break through those barriers and drive off the top of the bridge, plunging to a watery grave. Now whose fault would that be? It would be your own. You ignored the warnings. You were determined to do what you wanted to do in spite of the roadblocks that were erected for your own protection.

Know this: no one will be in hell or heaven by accident. That is why God sent Jesus—to provide us with God's gracious "roadblocks". If we reject them, the Bible asks, "How shall we escape if we neglect so great a salvation?" (Hebrews 2:3).

4. There are too many hypocrites in church!

We've all heard people say, "The reason I am not a Christian is because there are too many hypocrites in the church! When I find the perfect, hypocrite-free church, then maybe I'll join." All I can say is that if those people do find the perfect, "hypocrite-free" church, they shouldn't join it. They would only spoil it.

Sadly, there is a great deal of hypocrisy in the church today. You will find many people attending church who are pretending to be something they aren't. I heard the story of a man who was desperate to make some money, so he went down to the city zoo, hoping to get a job feeding the animals. The manager at the zoo had no openings, but seeing how big this man was, he offered him another possible position. "Our gorilla died the other day, and that was one of our most popular exhibits! If we got you a special gorilla suit, would you put it on and imitate him for a few days? We'll pay you well for it!"

The guy was so desperate he agreed. He actually did quite well over the next few days. He would dress up in his gorilla suit, beat his chest, and shake the bars of his cage. Huge crowds soon gathered at the exhibit. And the money was good. One day, however, while performing his gorilla act, he was swinging on his trapeze and accidentally lost his grip. This landed him right in the middle of the lion's den! The huge beast gave a ferocious roar. The man in the gorilla suit realized he couldn't cry for help without revealing that he was a fake. He slowly walked backward away from the lion, hoping to climb back into his cage. The lion, with a very hungry look on his face, started to follow him. Finally in desperation the man in the gorilla suit cried out, "Help!"

Immediately the lion whispered loudly, "Shut up, stupid! You'll get us both fired!"

Unfortunately, like the "pseudo-zoo" in this story, you will find hypocrites in the church today. You cannot deny that when confronted with this excuse. Yet you must also point out that just because someone attends a church does not necessarily mean that he or she is even a Christian! That hypocrite the unbeliever cites as an example may not even be a real follower of Jesus to start with. Then again, there are those who are true believers who have not lived the Christian life as they should.

It might not be a bad idea if we Christians wore a sign around our neck that said, "Under Construction." But I do know this: Jesus did not say, "Follow my people"; he said, "Follow me." He will never be a hypocrite. He will never be inconsistent. He will be all he promises to be in our life.

15

THE REAL REASON PEOPLE SAY NO AND WHAT TO DO ABOUT IT

The Bottom Line—The Need for Change

What is the real reason as opposed to the excuse? Jesus gave the answer in the third chapter of John's Gospel: "This is the verdict: Light has come into the world, but men loved darkness instead of light because their deeds were evil. Everyone who does evil hates the light, and will not come into the light for fear that his deeds will be exposed. But whoever lives by the truth comes into the light, so that it may be seen plainly that what he has done has been done through God" (John 3:19-21, NIV).

Many people just don't want to change. They want to continue as they always have. They may point to this or that excuse, but the bottom line is that they don't really want to change. But we must not give up on them.

I shared a story in the beginning of this booklet about the first person that I was able to lead to Christ. But I must tell you that I was not very bold about sharing my faith in the beginning.

A few days after I had received Christ on my high

school campus, I was sort of in a spiritual no-man's land. I was not really comfortable with the Christians on campus yet, and I had not been back to see my old friends since I had made this commitment. At lunchtime, I decided that I would go back and hang out with some of my old buddies, just for old times' sake. I certainly did not want to tell them about my newfound faith. I wanted to keep it as quiet as possible.

One of my friends had a house right next to our campus, so we would often hang out there at lunchtime. As I was making my way there, one of the Christians on campus recognized me and yelled out (very loudly, I might add), "Hey, brother Greg! Praise the Lord!"

"Yeah, right—uh, praise the Lord," I muttered.

"Hey, bro," this zealous Christian said, "I've got something for you!" He then proceeded to hand me a rather large Bible with a faded leather cover. Glued on the front of it were two Popsicle sticks in the shape of a cross! To be honest with you, I really did not want this Bible or this very public conversation with this outspoken Christian at that moment.

"Read it, and you will grow spiritually!" he promised.

"Uh, okay. Thanks. I'll do that," I sheepishly replied. After he left, I thought to myself, *What am I going to do with this Bible? I can't actually carry it publicly across campus. People will think I'm some kind of religious nut!*

So being the bold witness for Christ that I was, I proceeded to take the Bible with its Popsicle sticks in the shape of a cross on it and stuff it into my coat pocket. Because of the sheer size of it, this caused my pocket to rip.

I slowly made my way over to my friend's house and was ready to walk in when I remembered the Bible in my coat pocket. I didn't want my friends to see Greg Laurie carrying Scripture around, so I looked for some place to ditch it. There in front of my friend's house was a planter. I quickly looked both ways, hid my Bible under some leaves, and made my way inside. As I casually sauntered in, my friends seemed somewhat surprised to see me.

"Hey, Laurie, where ya been?"

"Nowhere," I said nonchalantly.

"Whatchya been doing?"

"Nothing," I said.

One of them said, "Hey, you wanna smoke some weed [marijuana] before class?"

Now, to be perfectly honest, if they had asked me that same question a few days earlier, I might have said yes. But it suddenly just didn't seem right. "No!" I said rather strongly, surprising even myself a little bit. All the time that this was going on, my heart was beating like a drum. It was as though I heard the Lord speaking to my heart saying, "Tell them about me." In response I was saying, "No! You tell them if you want to!"

Suddenly the front door burst open. There stood

my friend's mother with my Bible in her hand—
Popsicle sticks and all!

"Who does *this* belong to?" she demanded. Every
eye in the room looked at that Bible and then at me.
Somehow they just knew there was a connection.

"It's mine," I said very quietly.

"What is that, Laurie?" one of my buddies shouted
at me.

"It's a Bible," I said, again, very quietly.

"A *what?*" my buddies asked.

"A Bible! A B–I–B–L–E!"

One of them said very sarcastically, "Oh, praise the
Lord, brother Greg. Are we going to be good little
Christians now and read the Bible and go to church?"

I shot back, "No! We're going to hit you in the
mouth if you don't shut up!" (I had not yet read the
part about loving your neighbor in the Bible I was
hiding.) Needless to say, I was not a very bold witness
for Jesus Christ in the beginning. But it was not long
until I realized that I could not, as a Christian, live in
two worlds. Nor could I hide what God had so gra-
ciously done for me.

Becoming a Christian means changing—and
some people are just plain scared!

Keep Trying

There is an old proverb that says, "When you throw a
rock into a pack of dogs, the one that barks the loud-
est is the one that has been hit." Sometimes the people

who are the most argumentative and combative may actually be closer to coming to Christ than you may think.

There may be one person you are sharing the gospel with who is very kind about it when you speak to him or her. He or she may say things like, "Oh, I am so glad that you have found religion. You seem to be a lot happier than you used to be."

You might reply that it is not religion you have found but a personal relationship with Jesus Christ. You might ask that person to go to church with you, and he or she will sweetly say, "You know, I would really like to do that some time."

You may think to yourself, "This person is really close to coming to Christ." Maybe so, maybe not. Things are not always as they seem.

There might be someone else who is always giving you a hard time about the gospel. Every Monday at work or school, they barrage you with a bunch of new questions they dreamed up for you over the weekend. They may scream and yell, creating a big scene. But remember, "When you throw a rock into a pack of dogs . . ." In reality, the person who is so sweet and understanding when you share the gospel may be very far from the kingdom, while the person who is always creating a fuss, arguing, and generally giving you a hard time may be very close.

I recently had a conversation with a man who is now the leader of a Christian denomination. He told me of how he used to be this way. A faithful believer had been sharing with him for some time. This particular man would mock, cajole, harass, and deride this Christian day in, day out. But the Christian would not give up. So one day, this man went to church just to get this Christian off his back. I was sharing the gospel message from the Word of God that day, and this man came to Christ. So don't give up!

Step Out

Today Jesus continues to say, "The harvest is plentiful but the workers are few. Ask the Lord of the harvest, therefore, to send out workers into his harvest field" (Matthew 9:37-38, NIV). Notice that Jesus does not say to pray for more observers or more spectators or more complainers. He is asking that you pray for more laborers.

But we cannot honestly pray that prayer if we are not willing to do it—to step out and be those laborers. Unfortunately, it seems like the church today could be compared to a giant football game, with sixty thousand people in the stands watching while twenty-two people do all the work. We all stand on the sidelines and say, "Go, team! Go!" But God is saying, "I want you down on the field. I want you to carry the ball. I want you to be a part of what I am doing."

You may feel unqualified for the calling, but think of what Jesus did with the twelve disciples. When we think of these men, we often think of them as holy or special. Yet though they were gifted and dedicated, they were ordinary. Jesus did not call them because they were great. Their greatness was the result of the call of Jesus.

God wants to use you. He has a place for you, a part for you to play, a seed for you to sow, a call for you to answer, a fish for you to catch! Begin by asking God's Holy Spirit to stir your heart so that you can answer this desire and wish of Jesus. You may pray something like this: "Lord, let it start with me. Make me a laborer—a fisher of men and women in this sea of life. I don't know what I can do. I feel a bit like that kid in the Bible who just had the loaves and fish. Here is my lunch, Lord—it's not much, but I give it to you." If you pray that type of heartfelt prayer, just watch what God will do!

Leading people to Christ is the most joyful experience I know of next to having met him myself. I like the statement of C. H. Spurgeon, who said, "To be a soul winner is the happiest thing in this world. With every soul you bring to Jesus Christ you seem to get a whole new heaven on earth."

This is not a suggestion. This is not an option. It is a command. But it is a blessed command—and a tremendous privilege. So get out there, and start doing your part. Let's go fishing!